INTRODUCTION

The Pacific Northwest coast between Oregon and British Columbia is one of the richest areas in the world for intertidal life. Winds and currents act to continuously dredge up cold nutrient-rich waters from below. The plant life contained in these waters flourishes when exposed to the sun, and the plants attract plant-eaters and so on up the food chain.

The rocky coast is characterized by wind- and wave-sculpted arches, caves and towering sea stacks. Offshore islands are a haven for sea bird colonies and marine mammals including sea lions, seals, sea otters and killer whales. Tidepools flourish with life. The sandy coast harbors an abundance of small animals – clams, crabs and insects – that provide a feast for millions of shorebirds.

Before You Begin

- Ensure it is legal to beachcomb in the area.
- If you want to collect specimens, be aware of size and bag limits.
- Seashores, estuaries and marshes are the breeding grounds and nurseries for many sea animals. Treat the land and water with care and respect; disrupted/damaged areas can take decades to recover.

Beachcomber Gear

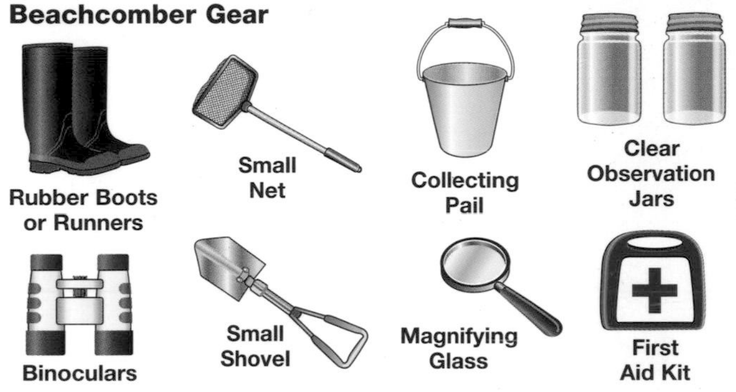

Rubber Boots or Runners
Small Net
Collecting Pail
Clear Observation Jars
Binoculars
Small Shovel
Magnifying Glass
First Aid Kit

> **PROTECT DUNES**
>
> They provide natural coastal protection and offer important coastal habitats. Avoid walking on or through them where possible, and where you can't, tread carefully.

Most animal illustrations show the adult male in breeding coloration. Colors and markings may be duller or absent during different seasons. Measurements refer to the length of animals and the height of plants unless otherwise indicated. Illustrations are not to scale.

N.B. – Never eat a wild animal or plant unless you are absolutely sure it is safe to do so. The publisher makes no representation or warranties with respect to the accuracy, completeness, correctness or usefulness of this information and specifically disclaims any implied warranties of fitness for a particular purpose. The advice, strategies and/or techniques contained herein may not be suitable for all individuals. The publisher shall not be responsible for any physical harm (up to and including death), loss of profit or other commercial damage. The publisher assumes no liability brought or instituted by individuals or organizations arising out of or relating in any way to the application and/or use of the information, advice and strategies contained herein.

Waterford Press publishes reference guides that introduce readers to nature observation, outdoor recreation and survival skills. Product information is featured on the website: **www.waterfordpress.com**

$7.95 U.S.
$9.95 CAN

ISBN 978-1-58355-557-6

Text & illustrations © 2010, 2023 Waterford Press Inc. All rights reserved. Photos © Shutterstock.

To order or for information on custom published products please call 800-434-2555 or email orderdesk@waterfordpress.com. For permissions or to share comments email editor@waterfordpress.com. 2306503

10 9 8 7 6 5 4 3 2 1

Made in the USA

A POCKET NATURALIST® GUIDE

PACIFIC NORTHWEST BEACHCOMBER

A Waterproof Folding Guide to Beach Habitats, Plants & Animals from Oregon to British Columbia

PACIFIC NORTHWEST BEACHCOMBER

T0123930

WATERFORD PRESS

COASTAL HABITATS

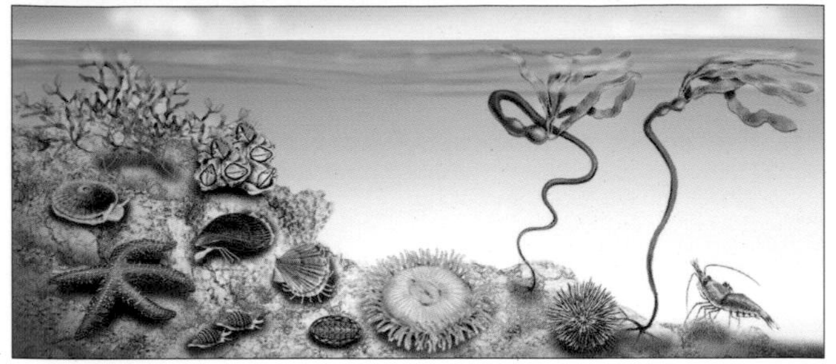

Rocky Shores

Many species inhabiting rocky shorelines have special adaptations that allow them to cling to rocks and withstand being pummelled by waves. Bull kelp have tangled roots called 'holdfasts' that anchor them to submerged rocks. Sea stars, anemones and limpets have sucker-like appendages that allow them to move about and cling to rocks. Barnacles and mussels cement themselves to rocks with sticky threads. When tides recede, rocky tidepools harbor a vast array of species that are easily observed.

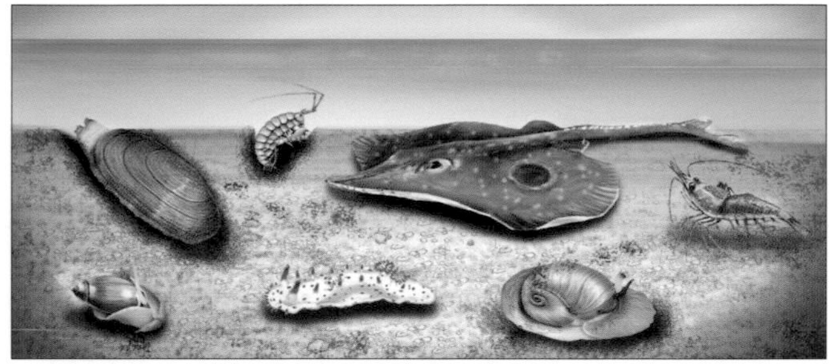

Sandy Shores

Animals found on sandy beaches and mudflats dig into the sand to protect themselves from predators. Their presence is often detected by dimples they leave in the surface of the sand as waves retreat. Bivalves like clams create small 'siphon' holes (a siphon is a fleshy tube-like structure which draws water into the shell). Sandy offshore waters are home to flounder and sole which camouflage themselves in the sand. Shoreline dunes are a fragile ecosystem that includes an array of grasses and plants which help to stabilize the sandy soil, including morning glories, tansies and verbenas.

> **PROTECT SEASHORE LIFE**
>
> - Watch where you are walking and try to avoid stepping on barnacles and other animals.
> - Avoid harming species' habitats by carelessly flipping over rocks. Gently turn over rocks and return them to their original position when done observing.
> - When looking for animals in seaweed, re-cover them with seaweed so they don't dry out.
> - Do not move animals out of their original habitat.
> - Many intertidal species are protected. As a rule, do not collect any live specimens unless you are certain it is legal to do so.

COASTAL HABITATS

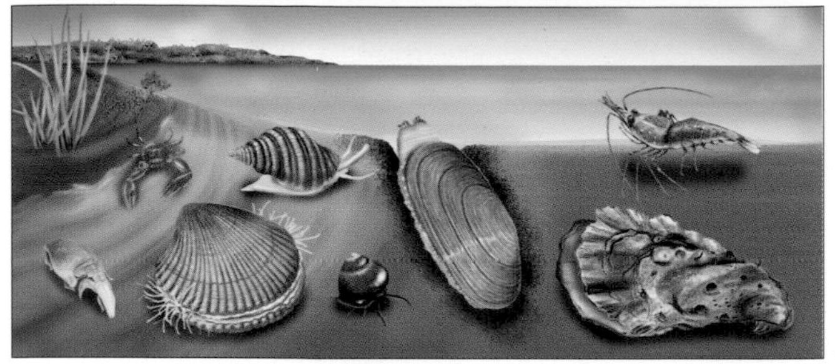

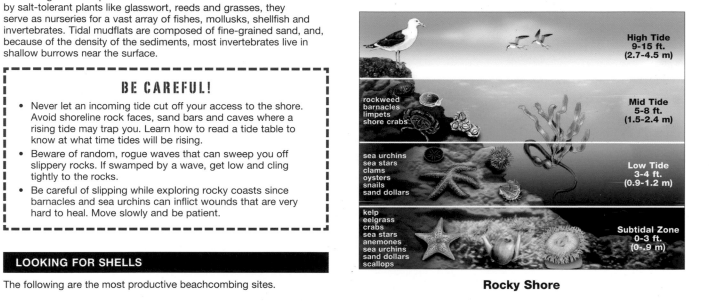

Tidal Marshes & Mudflats

Salt marshes form in bays and estuaries where salt and fresh water mix. These areas contain decomposing plant and animal matter and are among the most productive natural habitats on earth. Dominated by salt-tolerant plants like glasswort, reeds and grasses, they serve as nurseries for a vast array of fishes, mollusks, shellfish and invertebrates. Tidal mudflats are composed of fine-grained sand, and, because of the density of the sediments, most invertebrates live in shallow burrows near the surface.

> **BE CAREFUL!**
>
> - Never let an incoming tide cut off your access to the shore. Avoid shoreline rock faces, sand bars and caves where a rising tide may trap you. Learn how to read a tide table to know at what time tides will be rising.
> - Beware of random, rogue waves that can sweep you off slippery rocks. If swamped by a wave, get low and cling tightly to the rocks.
> - Be careful of slipping while exploring rocky coasts since barnacles and sea urchins can inflict wounds that are very hard to heal. Move slowly and be patient.

LOOKING FOR SHELLS

The following are the most productive beachcombing sites.

Driftlines

The wavy line of debris marking the high tide line is an excellent place to find the shells of mollusks. Look under the seaweed and driftwood for shells and the skeletons of crabs and sea urchins.

Piers and Pilings

Wooden piers and stone pilings provide an ideal habitat for a wide array of creatures including barnacles, mussels, sea stars, crabs and chitons.

Tidepools

When the tide goes out on rocky shores, pockets of seawater collect in pools that harbor communities of anemones, limpets, sea stars, sea urchins and even small fishes.

> **TIP** Rare shells and marine skeletons are often thrown up on beaches following storms.

TIDAL ZONES

There are generally two tides a day, and tidal differences may be as much as 55 ft. (16.5 m) – the Bay of Fundy – although high tide is typically between 9-15 ft. (2.7-4.5 m). The lowest tides of the year occur in midwinter and midsummer.

Seashore life is distributed in a number of life zones along shorelines. These zones are especially evident on rocky shores since animals live in different zones based on exposure to air, food availability, shelter and protection from predators.

Creatures living in high tide zones get wet by tides twice daily. Those in mid-tide zones are covered by water most of the time. Those in low tide zones are almost always submerged.

The best time to observe the greatest variety of species is during low tide. The highest and lowest tides occur every two weeks during the new (dark) moon or full moon. Tide times are often published in newspapers, and tide tables are available at most sporting goods stores.

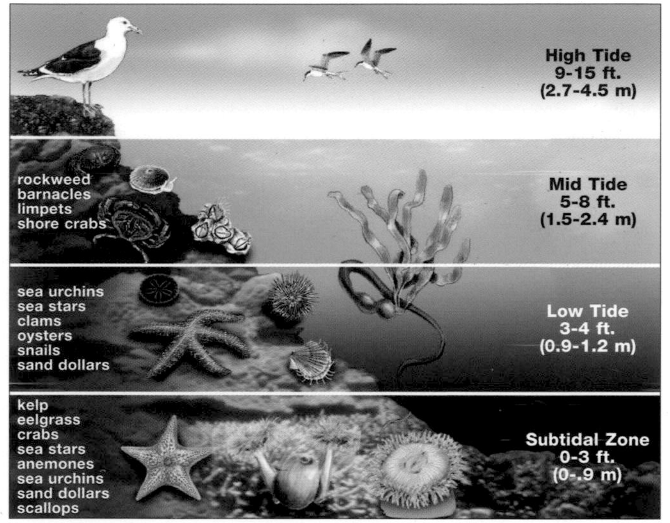

High Tide
9-15 ft.
(2.7-4.5 m)
rockweed
barnacles
limpets
shore crabs
Mid Tide
5-8 ft.
(1.5-2.4 m)
sea urchins
sea stars
clams
oysters
snails
sand dollars
Low Tide
3-4 ft.
(0.9-1.2 m)
kelp
eelgrass
crabs
sea stars
anemones
sea urchins
sand dollars
scallops
Subtidal Zone
0-3 ft.
(0-.9 m)

Rocky Shore

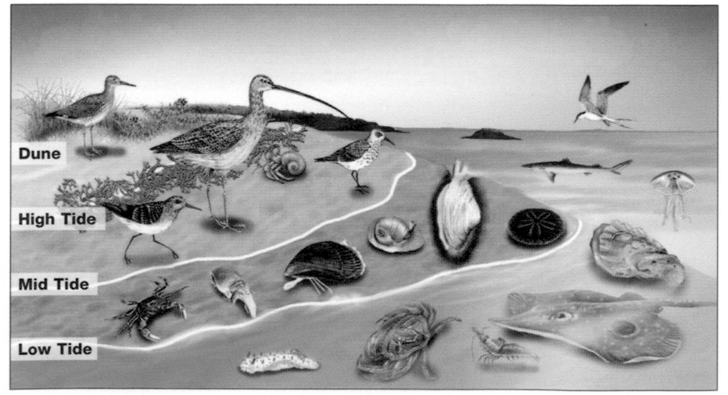

Dune
High Tide
Mid Tide
Low Tide

Sandy Shore

SEASHORE PLANTS

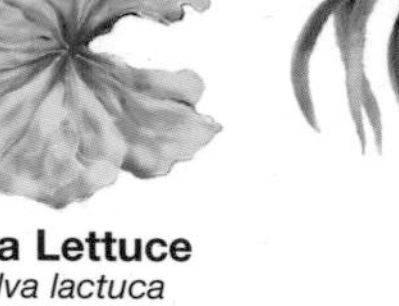

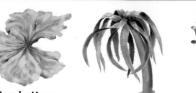

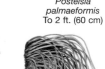

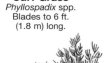

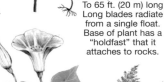

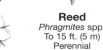

Sea Lettuce
Ulva lactuca
To 26 in. (65 cm)

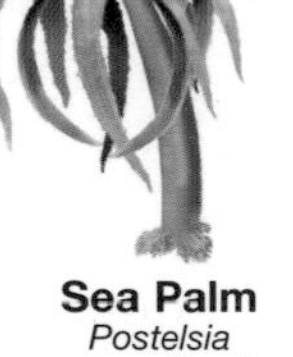

Sea Palm
Postelsia palmaeformis
To 2 ft. (60 cm)

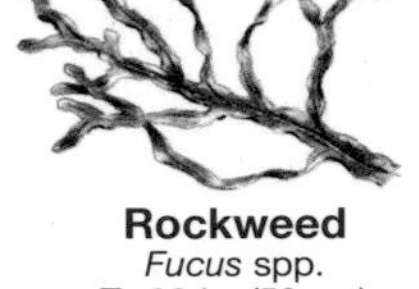

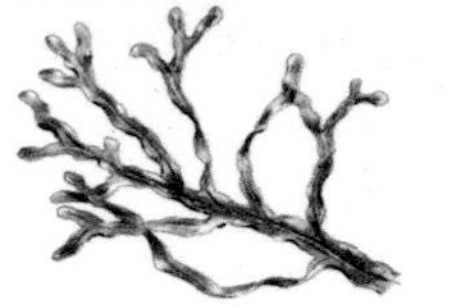

Rockweed
Fucus spp.
To 20 in. (50 cm)
Ribbed stem is covered with swollen air bladders.

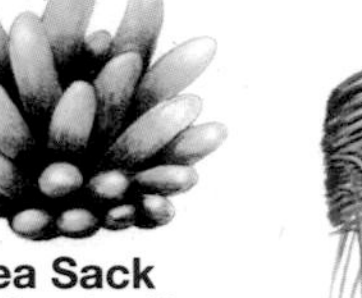

Sea Sack
Halosaccion glandiforme
To 4 in. (10 cm)

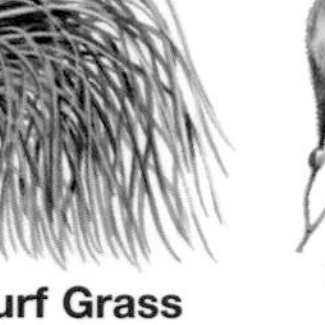

Surf Grass
Phyllospadix spp.
Blades to 6 ft. (1.8 m) long.

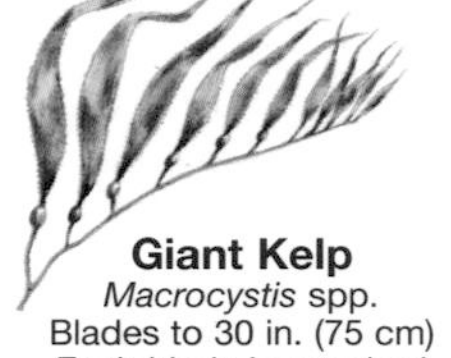

Giant Kelp
Macrocystis spp.
Blades to 30 in. (75 cm)
Each blade is attached to a round float.

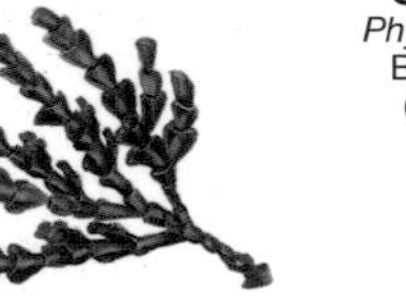

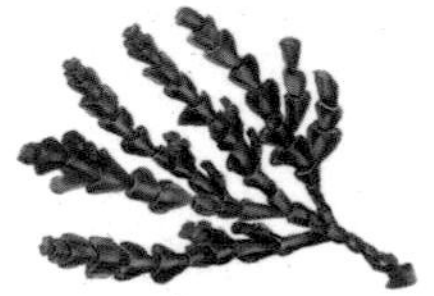

Coralline Seaweed
Calliarthron spp.
To 10 in. (25 cm)

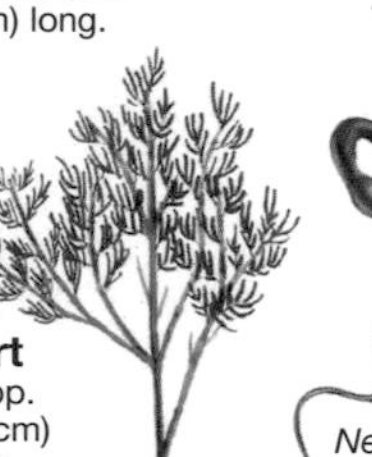

Glasswort
Salicornia spp.
To 18 in. (45 cm)
Common in salt marshes.

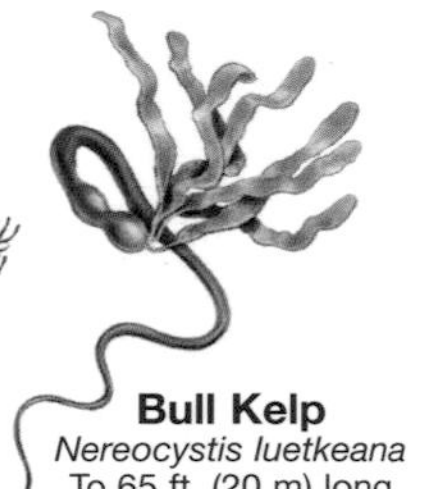

Bull Kelp
Nereocystis luetkeana
To 65 ft. (20 m) long
Long blades radiate from a single float. Base of plant has a "holdfast" that it attaches to rocks.

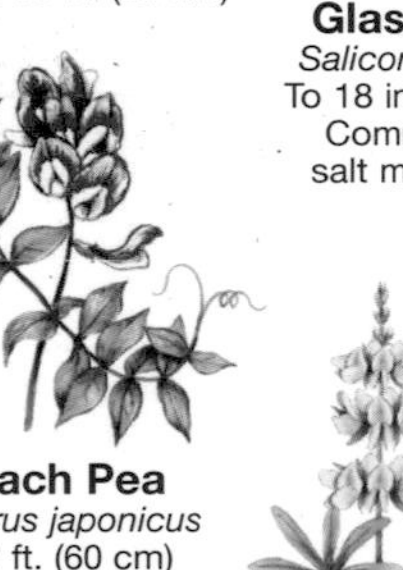

Beach Pea
Lathyrus japonicus
To 2 ft. (60 cm)
Creeping plant found on dunes and beaches.

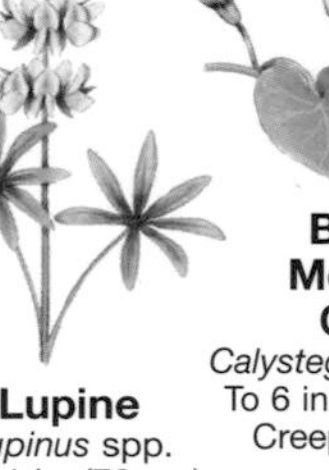

Lupine
Lupinus spp.
To 31 in. (78 cm)
Note star-shaped leaves.

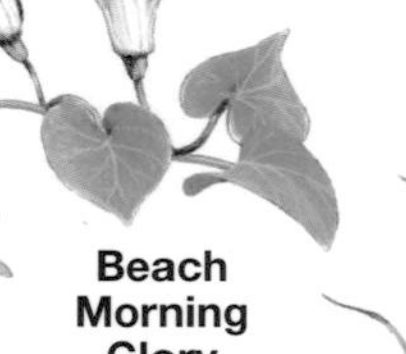

Beach Morning Glory
Calystegia soldanella
To 6 in. (15 cm) tall
Creeping plant.

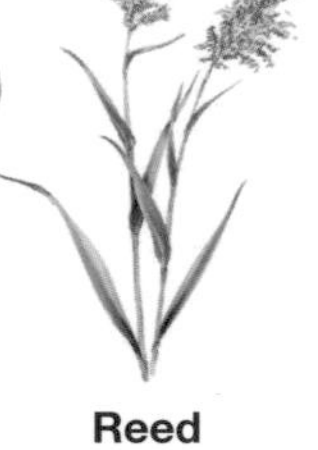

Reed
Phragmites spp.
To 15 ft. (5 m)
Perennial grass grows in brackish waters.

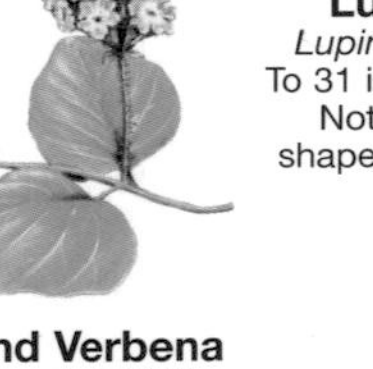

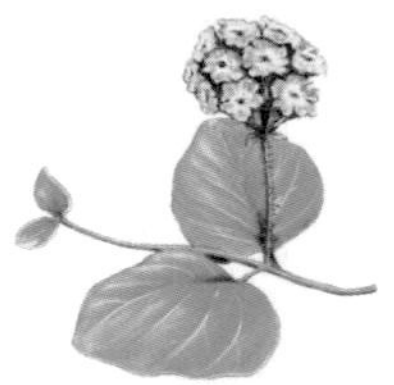

Sand Verbena
Abronia latifolia
To 6 in. (15 cm)

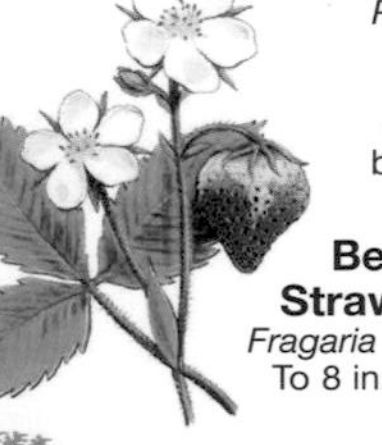

Beach Strawberry
Fragaria chiloensis
To 8 in. (20 cm)

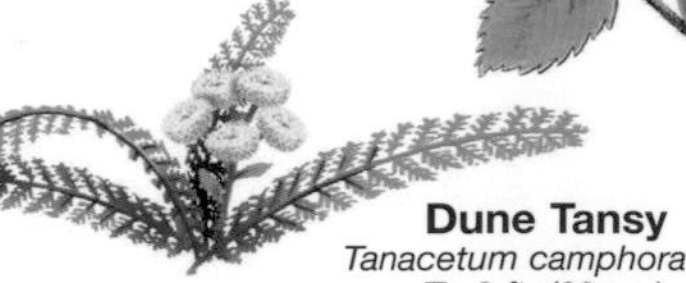

Dune Tansy
Tanacetum camphoratum
To 2 ft. (60 cm)

MOLLUSKS

This large group of soft-bodied and usually hard-shelled invertebrates occupy many habitats in water and on land. The mouth of most mollusks – excluding bivalves – has a ribbon-like toothed structure called a radula which helps the animals break down food or capture prey.

Limpets

Limpets have flat or conical one-part shells. They cling to rocks and feed by scraping algae from rocks with rasping "tongues."

Rough Keyhole Limpet
Diodora aspera
To 3 in. (8 cm)

Duncecap Limpet
Acmaea mitra
To 1 in. (3 cm)

Nudibranchs

Also called sea slugs, nudibranchs are essentially snails without shells. Found in tidepools.

Sea Clown Nudibranch
Triopha catalinae
To 6 in. (15 cm)

Spotted Nudibranch
Diaulula sandiegensis
To 3.5 in. (9 cm)

Snails

Most snails have a one-part spiral shell and are edible.

Black Turban Snail
Chlorostoma funebralis
To 1 in. (3 cm)

Dogwinkle
Nucella emarginata
To 1.5 in. (4 cm)

Purple Dwarf Olive
Olivella biplicata
To 1.25 in. (3.6 cm)

Frilled Dogwinkle
Nucella lamellosa
To 3 in. (8 cm)
Shell has erect frills.

Moon Snail
Euspira lewisii
To 3 in. (8 cm)

Giant Western Nassa
Nassarius fossatus
To 2 in. (5 cm)

Oregon Hairy Triton
Fusitriton oregonensis
To 5 in. (13 cm)
The largest snail in the region.

Abalones

Flattened snail is similar to a limpet but larger. Shell has 5 holes and a rough surface. A prized delicacy.

Northern Abalone
Haliotis kamtschatkana
To 6 in. (15 cm)

Chitons

Shell has 8 overlapping plates. Like limpets, they cling to rocks.

Lined Chiton
Tonicella lineata
To 2 in. (5 cm)

MOLLUSKS

Bivalves

All have two-part shells that are hinged. Most are edible. Red tides cause shellfish poisoning so be sure to check for seasonal closures, size and bag limits.

Blue Mussel
Mytilus edulis
To 4 in. (10 cm)
Smooth shell is blue, black or brown.

California Mussel
Mytilus californianus
To 10 in. (25 cm)
Shell has deep ridges.

Giant Pacific Oyster
Crassostrea gigas
To 12 in. (30 cm)

Heart Cockle
Clinocardium nuttallii
To 6 in. (15 cm)

Giant Pacific Scallop
Patinopecten caurinus
To 10 in. (25 cm)

Pacific Pink Scallop
Chlamys hastata
To 3 in. (8 cm)

Pacific Razor Clam
Siliqua patula
To 7 in. (18 cm)

Pacific Littleneck Clam
Protothaca staminea
To 3 in. (8 cm)

Soft-shelled Clam
Mya arenaria
To 6 in. (15 cm)

Geoduck (Gooey duck)
Panopea generosa
To 9 in. (23 cm)
The largest burrowing clam in the world has a long siphon up to 40 in. (1 m) long. Hundreds of millions inhabit Puget Sound.

> ### HARVESTING SHELLFISH
> - You need a license to harvest live shellfish.
> - There are harvesting seasons and bag limits.
> - Always check for closures due to pollution or harmful algal blooms (red tides).

Cephalopods

Have 8 or more "arms" positioned around the mouth.

Giant Pacific Octopus
Enteroctopus dofleni
To 5 ft. (1.5 m)

Opalescent Squid
Doryteuthis opalescens
To 12 in. (30 cm)

ECHINODERMS

These mostly bottom-dwelling animals are characterized by spiny bodies and radial symmetry, i.e., body parts repeat around a central hub. The "arms" are usually arranged in multiples of 5, and may be short or long, cylindrical or flattened. Size refers to width.

Sea Stars

Central disk is surrounded by 5-40 "arms." Suckers on bottom of arms facilitate motion and allow them to cling to rocks.

Ochre Sea Star
Pisaster ochraceus
To 20 in. (50 cm)
May be red, purple, orange or brown.

Six-rayed Star
Leptasterias spp.
To 4 in. (10 cm)

Sunflower Star
Pycnopodia helianthoides
To 52 in. (1.3 m)
Note huge size.

Daisy Brittle Star
Ophiopholis aculeata
To 9 in. (23 cm)

Mottled Sea Star
Evasterias troschelii
To 16 in. (40 cm)
Color varies from orange-brown to blue-gray.

Leather Star
Dermasterias imbricata
To 10 in. (25 cm)
Smells like garlic.

Pacific Blood Star
Henricia leviuscula
To 8 in. (20 cm)

Sea Urchins & Sand Dollars

Internal shell is covered with moveable spines of varying length. The shells (called tests) often wash up on beaches.

Purple Sea Urchin
Strongylocentrotus purpuratus
To 4 in. (10 cm)

Green Sea Urchin
Strongylocentrotus droebachiensis
To 3 in. (8 cm)

Sand Dollar
Dendraster excentricus
To 3 in. (8 cm)

BEACH DRIFT

Dogfish Egg Case

Skate Egg Case

Sand Dollar Shell

Sea Urchin Shell

COELENTERATES

This group contains a variety of free-swimming and colonial creatures including jellyfish, hydroids, anemones and corals.

Anemones

Flower-like animals have stinging tentacles near their tops that they use to subdue prey. When disturbed they retract their tentacles. Found in tidepools and on rocks and pilings.

Brooding Anemone
Epiactis prolifera
To 1.5 in. (4 cm)

Frilled Anemone
Metridium senile
To 18 in. (45 cm)

Giant Green Anemone
Anthopleura xanthogrammica
To 12 in. (30 cm)

Aggregate Anemone
Anthopleura elegantissima
To 20 in. (50 cm)
Usually grow in clumps.

Jellyfish

Bell-shaped animals often wash ashore after storms. Most have stinging tentacles and should never be handled.

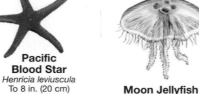 

Moon Jellyfish
Aurelia aurita
To 16 in. (40 cm)

By-the-wind Sailor
Velella velella
To 3 in. (8 cm)
Small crest on upper surface acts as a sail.

Sea Gooseberry
Pleurobrachia pileus
To 1 in. (3 cm) wide

Lion's Mane Jellyfish
Cyanea capillata
To 8 ft. (2.4 m)
Largest in the world.

NEARSHORE FISHES

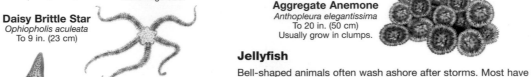

Tidepool Sculpin
Oligocottus maculosus
To 4 in. (10 cm)

Spiny Dogfish
Squalus acanthias
To 5 ft. (1.5 m)

Buffalo Sculpin
Enophrys bison
To 15 in. (38 cm)

Big Skate
Raja binoculata
To 8 ft. (1.5 m)
Nearshore fish is common in shallow water over soft bottoms.

ARTHROPODS

All have hard outer skeletons and paired, jointed appendages.

Dungeness Crab
Cancer magister
To 9 in. (23 cm)

Hermit Crab
Pagurus spp.
To 1.25 in. (3.6 cm)
Lives in discarded snail shells.

Red Crab
Cancer productus
To 6 in. (15 cm)

Kelp Crab
Pugettia producta
To 4 in. (10 cm)

Porcelain Crab
Petrolisthes cinctipes
To 1 in. (3 cm)

Pacific Mole Crab
Emerita analoga
To 1.5 in. (4 cm)
Moves up and down beaches with the tide.

Purple Shore Crab
Hemigrapsus nudus
To 2.5 in. (6 cm)

Barnacle
Balanus spp.
To 3 in. (8 cm)
Grows in clusters on rocks and piers.

Beach Hopper
Megalorchestia californiana
To 1.25 in. (3.6 cm)
Tiny crustaceans are found in seaweed debris.

Coon-striped Shrimp
Pandalus danae
To 6 in. (15 cm)
Often seen around pilings.

Leaf Barnacle
Pollicipes polymerus
To 3.5 in. (9 cm)

MARINE MAMMALS

Harbor Seal
Phoca vitulina
To 6 ft. (1.8 m)

Northern Sea Lion
Eumetopias jubatus
To 10.5 ft. (3.2 m)

Sea Otter
Enhydra lutris
To 6 ft. (1.8 m)

Killer Whale
Orcinus orca
To 30 ft. (9 m)

SHOREBIRDS

       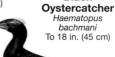       

Sanderling
Calidris alba
To 8 in. (20 cm)
Runs in and out with waves along shorelines.

Willet
Tringa semipalmata
To 17 in. (43 cm)

Greater Yellowlegs
Tringa melanoleuca
To 15 in. (38 cm)

Western Sandpiper
Calidris mauri
To 7 in. (18 cm)

Spotted Sandpiper
Actitis macularius
To 8 in. (20 cm)

Long-billed Curlew
Numenius americanus
To 26 in. (65 cm)
Long bill is slightly downturned.

Black Turnstone
Arenaria melanocephala
To 9 in. (23 cm)

American Avocet
Recurvirostra americana
To 20 in. (50 cm)

Black Oystercatcher
Haematopus bachmani
To 18 in. (45 cm)

Black-crowned Night-Heron
Nycticorax nycticorax
To 28 in. (70 cm)

Great Blue Heron
Ardea herodias
To 4.5 ft. (1.4 m)

Double-crested Cormorant
Phalacrocorax auritus
To 3 ft. (90 cm)
Note orange-yellow throat patch.

Ring-billed Gull
Larus delawarensis
To 20 in. (50 cm)
Has dark ring.

Western Gull
Larus occidentalis
To 27 in. (68 cm)
Large gull has a dark back.

Common Tern
Sterna hirundo
To 15 in. (38 cm)